Healing
with
Seichim/Reiki

by
Maurice Ramsey

Llumina Press

ISBN: 1-932047-96-4
Printed in the United States of America

ACKNOWLEDGMENT

I wish to thank Elisa Street and Harry Schwab for their assistance in editing this book.

I am very grateful to the many guides, angels, archangel healers, my guardian angels and master teachers who continue to provide their guidance, light, wisdom, love, and support in many endeavors. Special thanks go to my daughter Idwona Ramsey and her Guides for her loving support and insight. I thank the Source All-That-Is for this life that I AM.

Table of Contents

A NOTE TO THE READER

*T*his is an instructional guide to help the advanced practitioner and the novice to understand the difference between Seichim and Reiki forms of healing. We will focus on Seichim and how Seichim can help develop intuitive and healing ability.

In this booklet, there are some of my experiences within my 35 years in the healing arts. My style of healing connects two worlds: man's and the spirit's. What I have learned as a result of my healing experiences is directly through the teaching and guidance of my *guardian angels*, *master teachers* and my *healing guides*. As a Seichim Reiki/Master Teacher, I was Divinely instructed to put some of my teaching on paper and the result is this booklet.

Seichim is derived from an ancient Egyptian form of healing. This method has proven to be extremely effective in treating minor discomforts, stress-related disorders, and chronic illnesses. Seichim helps strengthen and quicken the body's own healing resources and gives comfort to the terminally ill.

It is my hope that this booklet will aid in the search for an effective, loving, healing art: "Seichim." May your journey be an enjoyable one!

-Maurice

INTRODUCTION TO
SEICHIM/REIKI

S eichim (pronounced "say-keem") means Living Light and is an ancient Egyptian system of healing wisdom.

Sometimes Seichim is spelled; Seichim, Sekhem or SKHM, although some believe each spelling is related to different forms of energy healing.

Seichim and Reiki are similar, but the *practitioner* brings in a slightly different energy. In Reiki, the practitioner uses the Universal Life Energy that permeates and sustains our world. The practitioner who connects to the Universal Intelligence is able to focus on the symbol that is most needed for healing.

Whereas Reiki is described as the White Light, Seichem is the Rainbow —both from the same place, but very different in experience. Seichem is gentle and creative. Seichem opens up the psychic centers and students begin to work closely with various beings of the light. It depends on the practitioner and his ability to access the energy of the Source.

In Seichim, the practitioner learns to go beyond the symbols and connect to the Source, God All-That-Is. The practitioner knows he is not doing the healing, but it is the Source that works through the practitioner. It is God in action through the practitioner.

Some students and practitioners may have difficulty understanding the **"I AM PRESENCE."** As each soul takes on a body of flesh, it is the God-Self extended into that body. My Higher Self stated long ago, "Do not think of Me as an entity, you have done this for too long. I Am the Self of you, the GOD of your own BEING and you are never separated from me."

What is the Light or Living Light? When I speak of the Light or the Living Light, it is in all-encompassing terms. Within the Light, are the love, attributes, power, virtues, and aspects of the Creator, All-That-Is. The Living Light of the Creator is who one is as a Being of Light encased in the body.

INTRODUCING YOU TO YOUR GUIDES

*I*n the first step to becoming a Seichim Master Teacher, the student needs to be introduced to his *guardian angels*. The *guardian angels* and *master teacher* are present to guide the student through life lessons and to help awaken consciousness to help keep the student on life path toward Mastery.

This has been spoken many times before and might seem repetitious, but the student must realize that his *guardian angel's* and *master teacher's* mission has been to help the student become aware of his "I AM" or his God-Self. The *guardian angel's* mission is to help the student connect to the God-Self so that he is able to learn and teach from the I AM Center of himself.

The Seichim Master will help empower the student, allowing the instrument of Light to flow through him and assist him in this earthly plain.

Method of Attunement

- The *practitioner* will open with a short prayer and call Living Light to enfold the *student*.

- The *student* should be standing, arms at his side, taking a few deep breaths to calm the body.

- The *practitioner* will then cleanse and balance the aura.

- The *practitioner* will ask the student to raise his arms up close to his sides, arms extend outward, palms faced upward ready to receive their *guardian angel* energies.

- The *practitioner* will ask God permission to call in the *guardian angel* to make the connection with the student.

- The *practitioner* will then asked the student to say out loud "God, please permit my *guardian angels* to come to me" or "God, please permit my *guardian angel* to connect with me".

- The *student* will wait for a few moments, then the *student* will feel a vibration or an energy that is different from his own; the *student* will realize this is his *guardian angel* connecting with him.

This is the first attunement for the Seichim Master Teacher to help the student connect to his *guardian angels.* These angels will help to bring in other energies that the student will need to help connect to his *master teachers* and *healing guides.* It is the Seichim energies that help the student become more aware of the power within.

The practitioner can use the same method in introducing the student to healing guides on page 18 *(Seichim Healing Session).* The energies will be different from their *guardian angel's* vibration as the spirit makes the contact with the student.

OPENING THE THIRD EYE

*T*he second attunement will open and activate the Third Eye through the Crown, Throat, and Heart centers, by sending Seichim (Living Light Energies) through these centers. This will help improve meditations and psychic abilities and bring more Light to the student.

In this exercise the Seichim Master Teacher will again empower the student. With the student's eyes closed the practitioner will place the right hand over the student's third eye. The left hand will be placed behind the back of the student's head while the practitioner sends forth the Seichim energies through the third eye to open the spiritual eye.

Next, the Practitioner will start calling in Light to the student; if the student cannot see the light, the practitioner should just ask the student to feel or visualize the Light so he will be conscious of it. The practitioner will say something like this: "You will feel the Living Light Energy of *pink light* coming from above into the crown of your head". Now the practitioner will ask the student to "pull the Light Energy down into the heart center and hold it there for a few moments". The student will feel the light opening and expanding within his heart and throughout his body. Next the practitioner will ask the student to bring the light up into his third eye or the mind's eye. The student will begin to see and feel the light opening and expanding throughout his body. The student will feel peace, joy and harmony within. This is the opening and cleansing process of the third eye.

With the eyes closed, the practitioner directs the student to sit, adjust his posture comfortably, with hands on the lap and palms up. The practitioner asks the student to relax his mind and body, and begin to take a few deep breaths, and call light to himself. Light is a Living Consciousness of God that responds instantly to the call; it is the Healing Light that opens and cleanses. It is the Healing Energies of the Source's Love in action within.

The practitioner directs the student to concentrate on each color, pink, blue, violet and white. The practitioner tells the student to look at each color in his mind's eye. If the student cannot see the colors, the student should feel or visualize each color, knowing they are there and become one with the color.

- **Pink:** Pink is the highest color ray of the Red family, the color of love. Red mixed with white completes the circle or root chakra, which is physical; the white ray is the crown chakra and is spiritual. The Pink ray is pure and unselfish love essence, which heals, perfects, and fulfills all life.

- **Green:** Green is the healing ray. It is health, balance, and harmony.

- **Blue:** The blue ray is the light of a medium. It is the color of spiritualization. It is the bridge between two worlds, man and spirit. It fills the mind with peace, joy, harmony and love.

- **Violet:** Violet is the ray of Self Mastery on the highest plane. It is Knowledge.

- **White:** White is the ray of perfection. It becomes one with the white light, signifying one with the God-Self or the Higher Self.

NOTE: With eyes still closed the practitioner should lead the student into meditation, entering with intent to connect to your Mighty I AM Presence. It is the gateway to the Universal Consciousness of God. The student will begin to see a beautiful light in the mind's eye, flow with the light, and become one with the light. This is your God-Self.

DEVELOP YOUR HEALING GIFT

*I*n the third attunement the practitioner will open and increase the energy in the Heart Center and activate the energy in the palms and fingertips by sending Seichim through these centers. The student receiving the third attunement will notice the sensations in his hands, like cold or warm feeling, light electrical prickles or waves of cool energy running through his hands.

Seichim is available to all who desire to connect with the Universal Life Energy of the Source. To become a practitioner and master teacher for healing, the student must meditate daily or every other day with the intention to reach the Higher Self. Seichim helps to open the doorway to the Higher Self. With the help of Master Teachers and Guardian Angels, the practitioner is instructed to empower the student to help raise his vibration ability to feel and meet with the healing guides. The student's healing guides will take advantage of the opportunity to introduce themselves to the students.

Once attunement is received, practice daily meditation of fifteen to twenty minutes on at least three to four days a week. This will help unify the chakras in the body, develop spiritual awareness, and bring the new energies together.

After the attunement there will be a weeklong cleansing process. In this period all chakras will be cleansed. The student may feel physical and mental reactions of lightness and a tingling in the crown of the head, heart, and hands. This is normal after an attunement. Daily treats and drinks of water are appropriate. The student should listen closely to the signal from the body, especially the heart, while the student is being fine-tuned.

God is simple! There is nothing difficult or mysterious about God. When meditating, the student should feel God within the center of the heart as a beautiful light within. Become one with the Light, the Light is within, around, above, and below. It is the Light of YOU, the God Self. All things are composed of the Light of God. The Light is within all things; there is nothing made that is without the Light of God. When speaking of the Light, it is an all-encompassing term. Within the Light are all the love, wisdom, power, virtues, and attributes of our Father God All-That-Is. The Light of the Source is who you really are.

The source of all ability lies within the heart center which is where the presence of God can be felt and trigger your psychic abilities and give inner sight. It can also increase sensitivity to the presence of the guardian angels, healing guides, ascended master, and master teachers. Seichim is the energies of Love, Power, Compassion; it is the Living Light Energies of the Source, All-That-Is. With the help of God's healing angels they are able to diagnose the problems of the patient and transmit Seichim energies through the practitioner to the problem areas of the patient's body. The healing angels are always ready to assist in the healing work of God. It is they who in God's name use their wisdom and the forces at their command to help take away pain, loosen locked joints, rebuild tissues. and bring peace and harmony to the body. The whole reason for Seichim is to touch the soul of the patient and bring health and harmony to the physical body.

MAURICE ON MEDITATION

S o let us begin. In meditation one must enter in the silence of meditation with intention to connect to the Higher Self. So I would suggest that you make your intention known. It is very important to make a practice of stating silently your intentions and desires. Call upon the master within. Call upon your higher Self. Believe me the manifestation of your own Higher Self is not any lesser a manifestation than that of Jesus or any of the angelic hosts. You must learn to reprogram yourself and call upon your own Higher Selves, your own God-self, the Mighty I AM Presence. This can be a rather profound experience. I ask you, please make your desire known, connect with the desire in your heart, and let it be sincere. Say a prayer; this sets the foundation. It does more good to sit and state your intention than simply to sit in the meditation position and continue to think about whatever comes into your mind. Break your old pattern and call upon the utmost mastery within to assist you in focusing.

I must make this clear: I understand that some of you have been practicing for a long time. You have worked effectively and allowed yourselves to be transformed. There is an opportunity now to give yourselves entirely to the Living Light of Love, to the Presence of your Higher Selves, and merge with it. Place no limitation upon yourself, for your Higher Self knows no limitation!

I will give you an affirmation that is *quite powerful,* and will assist you to reach a higher state of consciousness. This is one of the "I AM" affirmations.

With your eyes still closed, take a few deep breaths and repeat this silently to yourself. "I AM THE RESURRECTION AND THE LIFE." Feel the warm vibrations in your heart and in the middle of your chest. Stop and sense how you feel.

If you find it difficult to concentrate, or you hear your mind wandering, use either affirmation "I AM THE RESURRECTION AND THE LIFE" or "I AM ONE WITH THE LIGHT." The meaning: RESURRECTION means Light, LIGHT means Knowing, Knowing means Knowledge and Knowledge IS the wisdom of God. The I AM statement is a powerful affirmation of your own Higher Self. The I AM is God, in action, in you. Use these tools; they are for your pleasure and for your focus.

There is a presence in the center of your heart. If you focus upon your breath, and breathe light through the center of your heart you will feel the Presence that is behind the breath. This Presence is driving the breath. It is called the Holy Breath, which flows through every cell of your body. It's the presence of GOD, your God-Self, an energy pre-existent to speech and the very foundation of the Universe. The Presence is within you and each and every one who reads my words.

There is also light that you will see in your meditation from time to time. This light helps to open your third eye, not your physical eyes but your spiritual eye. This third eye is your true Self and your divinity. The light that you are is the light of God. So, my brothers and sisters just align with your breath and feel the Presence of God within the center of your HEART.

As you awaken the third eye center, you will receive much more clarity and guidance within. When you open up your heart chakra, all the other chakras will follow and allow you to connect more clearly and profoundly with your guides than you have previously. Remember, focus on your heart, and be conscious of your breathing and viewing the light within your third eye.

Step-by-Step for Meditation:

Before you enter into your meditation find a quiet place where you will not be disturbed. Next, the practitioner should say a short prayer, and invite God to come into your heart and mind.

The practitioner must open the four upper chakras *(The crown, third eye, throat and heart chakras)* before entering into meditation to receive the energies.

I would like you to follow these steps in connecting with your Higher Self.

- Sit with your eyes closed. Adjust your posture so that you feel comfortable, putting your hand on your lap, palms up. Begin by taking a few deep breaths.
- Now I want you to imagine your entire body feeling relaxed, starting with your feet, calves, and thighs, then up into your abdomen, lower back, chest and shoulders. Next relax your arms, hands, neck, and face. Let the muscles around your jaws and eyes feel very relaxed. Do this until you feel peaceful and physically comfortable.
- Adjust your posture so that your energy can flow more easily up and down your spine. Watch your breath; breathe into your upper chest several times; notice how you feel.

- Call Seichim to yourself. (This is the Living Light of God). Feel the light entering into your Temple and breathe light through your heart center, feel your heart start to open up into a beautiful ball of Light and allow yourself to expand.

- Fix your attention at the point between the eyebrows and ask God to come into your heart, while at the same time you will start to feel a glow, a warm feeling within the heart center. As you begin to feel the Presence of God, you should feel the Presence of a beautiful white light within, becoming one with the white light. If you can't see the white light, just feel the white light, but know that it is there. Contemplate God's attributes; God is all loving, all-powerful, so just flow with your feelings

- Ask God, "God, please help me to connect to my Higher Self." Imagine that you are being joined by many high Beings of the Light who are sitting in a circle around you. Feel their peace, joy, and love all around you. These Beings of Light are here to assist you in connecting with your Higher Self.

- Imagine your Higher Self in the distance, beginning to come towards you. You might picture it as a beautiful, shimmering, radiant light, greeting and welcoming you. Mentally ask your Higher Self to assist you in making a stronger connection. Feel the radiance of love from your Higher Self, surrounding you and embracing you.

- Now imagine your Higher Self taking you by your hands and transporting you to a space in time, where you are able to learn from your Higher Self. Your Higher Self can give you advice about any situation. Imagine that you are a wise teacher or a consultant and what advice you will give yourself. You may ask about your spiritual growth or your higher purpose in this life.

- In this state of consciousness you are able to do many things. You can send energy to your friends; you can help heal Mother Earth and yourself. Remember in this state you can see many forms of Light Beings around you. You may speak to your Master Teacher and ask them if they would like to give you a message. Your Higher Self is your Teacher.

- You have effectively met your Higher Self. Any time you need to know anything, just go within your Temple and connect with your Higher Self. It is the doorway to the Universal Consciousness, God All-That-Is.

Seichim Healing Session

*I*n most Seichim healing sessions, the Practitioner will place his hands slightly above the head and scan down and around the body, locating negative energies or the ill parts of the body. His hands may feel cool to the touch but will generate an enormous amount of heat as the healing angels start to channel Seichim energies through the practitioner into the patients. Some patients may experience sensations of being re-energized.

Other physical sensations include warmth or coolness. Some will feel extremely relaxed, and others may feel tingling sensations. This is a sure sign that the healing is working. It often takes a few moments to readjust to the world after a Seichim session.

Seichim healing is helpful on one level or another. Sometimes one treatment is sufficient, but often several are needed and the benefits emerge gradually. With some patients a successful outcome to healing is obvious, but for others, change takes place at a more subtle level and sometimes in an unexpected way. Seichim often helps with the speed and extent of recovery from serious illness and major surgery and from the effects of treatments such as chemotherapy and radiation therapy. Usually patients feel more stable, relaxed, and often experience a beneficial change in their attitude to life, a situation which often arises in the cases of terminal illness where healing brings serenity to the patient.

As the practitioner becomes an instrument of **God's** divine healing power, the Seichim Master will be filled with the healing vibration of God, from the top of the head to the soles of the feet. A beautiful, radiant white light that vibrates over the body will surround the practitioner. Most Ministers today say that they are filled with the Holy Spirit when they are performing their rituals (Laying-on-hands.) But the truth is, when the Minister invokes the healing prayers for the sick he is in contact with the Healing Angels of God. Therefore, the Minister is attuned, receiving healing energies from the healing angels, which God had set in motion from the beginning of time.

If you can, observe the healing hands of the angels as they go about their healing work, unblocking those blocked areas that are causing discomfort, taking away the pain, loosening locked joints, rebuilding tissues, bring peace and harmony to the body. You must understand, it not just one or two healing angels that are assisting Seichim Masters; there's a team of specialists and medical spirit doctors that are working on the other side, although they never incarnate in the physical world. But they are lending their love, light, and energy to help mankind improve their health and well-being.

There are some medical professionals and the Seichim Masters that have passed into the spirit world; they are still working at the task they love to serve, helping to heal the physical body. But **most importantly**, they are able to work on a broader scale. They are not limited in their healing work as they were on the earth in the physical body. In the spirit world they can see the source of the problem, and if it is God's will they can touch the spirit of the patient and help ignite the divine spark that can grow in illumination and strengthen the physical body.

If only you could see the chemical changes taking place in the mental, physical, and spiritual bodies of man, as spirit applies the Seichim energies of spiritual sounds, color rays, and the Living Light of the Source, GOD All-That-Is, then you would understand what Seichim is all about. Realize that GOD and YOU are ONE and you are the Light and God is the Source of the Light and know it is God in action through you.

EGYPTIAN ANCIENT FORM OF HEALING

Bring the index fingers and thumbs together creating a pyramid shape

*W*hen you form your hands in a pyramid shape, you are utilizing an ancient Egypt healing technique which dates back to 3 B.C. This method had been forgotten in time. *My master guides* revealed to me this ancient form of healing some 20 years ago, and ever since, I have been using this technique with excellent results.

When you bring your two hands together and form a pyramid shape, you can see the energies flowing through the middle of the pyramid shape of your hands. This style of healing is a very powerful one. You do not need to touch the client's body with your hands; all you need to do is place your hands about 14 inches from the client's body. Then, just concentrate on the part that is in need of healing. You will feel an enormous amount of energy flowing through the center of your hands into the client's body. Just close your eyes and become one with the Source of your I AM Presence and your thoughts alone will activate this remarkable healing energy that will flow through you.

Dear Students, Friends and Colleagues:

Anybody can become a Seichim or Reiki Master and use the symbols, crystals, etc…for healing. These are tools to help the Novices generate energy, which is good, but that is only the beginning of mastering the true knowledge and powers that come from within.

A true Master does not become a master over night. It takes years, and for most a lifetime. In this handbook I have provided you with some of the tools to help you on your journey to become a Master.

I would like for you to understand the Seichim Energy and who you really are. You are GOD, Co-Creator of God the Father. All of what GOD is you ARE. You must understand, you are an extension of God. God took of His Light (Seichim the Living Light) and made you. Within Seichim are all the love, wisdom, power, virtues, and attributes of the Source. SEICHIM is the Living Light of the Source; that is who you really are. God made you in His own image and Likeness.

Your I AM Presence is the extension of GOD your God-Self, which is a multidimensional spirit. That is able to function on many different levels (dimensions) at the same time. Your I AM Presence took a part of His consciousness and extended it into the earth plane where it takes on a physical body.

Know that you have the power to heal. Know that you are an extension of God Light and God work through you. You have all the power of Seichim and the Love of the Source within you.

Know every man can achieve Mastery as he learns and uses the Law. As he becomes the law unto himself, call on the Seichim energy for healing yourself, the Planet and others. The healing techniques that I have shown you above were revealed to me some twenty years ago and they are easy to use. Just know in your heart and mind that you are the extension of GOD and Seichim The Living Light flows through you.

I will close with this thought in mind, for you to feel the power from within you. Close your eyes and take a few deep breaths with intent (To feel the Source within YOU), then say five times slowly to your self. *"IT IS, GOD IN ACTION THROUGH ME."* Yes I know that you could feel the vibration within you. That comes by knowing that you are ONE with the SOURCE. This is one of the affirmations that I use in my healing and meditations.

This is one of my Healing Techniques:

- Close your eyes, relax your body, and invoke the Seichim energies as you attune to the spirit within, (Your Mighty I AM Presence, the God-Self).

- As you recognized the spirit within, you will declare. "God Is, I AM and we are One."

- Feel the energy in your Heart as you become one with the spirit within.

- Then you should say,, "Father use me for thine healing." Or, "Father, let thine will be done through me for their healing." (Use your own words; this is just a guide for you)

- You will feel an enormous amount of energy around your head. This is your Crown Chakra starting to open up to receive the Seichim energies.

- The Seichim energy will travel down into your third eye. You will see a beautiful with Light within you. You might feel the presence of the healing angels, as they are ready to assist you in the healing.

- The Seichim will continue traveling downward toward your spine into the Throat Chakra, opening up speech on the highest plane.

- The Seichim energy will travel into your Heart Chakra, opening up an enormous amount of healing energy that will flow down your arms into the hand shaped as a pyramid. Some will be able to see the white light generate from within their heart and outwardly around their body.

- You must remember it is God in action in through you. When Jesus performed the healing he stated, "It is not I that do the healing but it is the Father that dwells within me that Heals you."

- Place your hands about 14 inches above the body. The Seichim energy knows what to do and where to go. You are always guided through the spirit within. Just trust yourself.

- A true Master gives himself completely over to the Source, GOD, because he knows GOD IS and I AM and WE are ONE.

This is only one of the healing techniques that I use, but when you are one with the spirit within your Higher Self will take over; that is the true miracle, becoming one with the self. That is how it was from the beginning.

What I had learned many years ago you too can learn. It is easy; just open your heart and trust within the spirit, it is your God-Self of YOU.

I am sharing my experience with you that I had received from my Guides and Higher Self, for you to go out and share with others how to heal and grow in the Light and service of God. Most important, teach them how to go into the silent of meditation with intent and make the connection to the spirit within. This is where the power is.

Sincerely my Brothers & Sisters of the Light,

Maurice

TWELVE SOUL EXTENSIONS

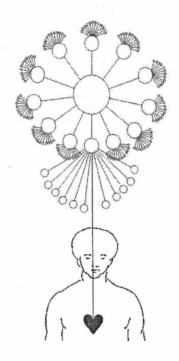

Soul extended into earth dimension
The "I AM is the Creative Spirit of The Universe

*K*now that the I AM Presence is you, your GOD-SELF which is a part of GOD. God made you in his own image and likeness.

Know that you are an extension of God; there is no separation from God. God lives within you and you in

God. God extended part of himself to create you, the I AM Presence, your God-Self that knows only Love, unconditional love, and what is right and perfect for you.

The I AM (God-Self) has the capability of expanding and expressing itself into twelve souls. Yes, twelve souls. Not only twelve souls— it has the capability of creating itself into twelve souls groups that have the ability to extend each soul at the same time into other dimensions of realities. What I am saying, your I AM has the capability to manifest yourself 144 times into different dimension, planets, and parallel universes of reality. This is your power; this is the power of God.

Seichim the Living Light of the Source

Seichim, the Living Light of GOD, is all encompassing and is everywhere present. It is the Glue (LOVE) that holds the Universe together. It is now, IS, ever has been, and ever shall BE. Seichim that IS, manifesting in and through All things and through which all things have come into expression. It is GOD in action.

All healing comes from within the heart center, it is Seichim, the Living Light of God's love, wisdom, power, virtues, and attributes that heal.

The I AM extended part of his conciseness into the earth dimension, to experience his realty in the third dimension. But you forgot your power, Seichim and your relationship with the Spirit within.

To make the connection to the I AM Presence, you must meditate within the heart center. Through meditation, you are able to open the door to Seichim and claim your birthright, to know that you are the Co-Creator with God.

When you invoke the healing energies it is Seichim the Living Light that manifested and radiated within the heart center. It's God expressing his Love and Light through you for healing.

SPIRITUAL CLEANSING FOR YOUR HOME, WORK PLACE & SELF

*I*t is a good idea to cleanse your house monthly as needed spiritually. Have you ever wondered why in most religious ceremonies the "priest" always burns incense in his place of worship after every service? When you were a child, do you remember the boogeyman in the closet? Are your children afraid of the dark or frightened to go down the stairs by themselves?

This is a sign that your house needs spiritual cleansing. You have negative entities in your home that feed off negativity surrounding you. Once these entities find a home with problems or children, they love to remain and attach themselves to you and your loved ones. They are called **Shadow People.** They hide in clutter, or dark corners, or in the closet where you place some of your undesirable things. They love to cause troubles because they feed off the trouble they create.

Everyone, at some time or another, has met an individual who seems to be surrounded with negativity, or has visited a place that seems to be filled with bad vibrations. These entities feed off of places like these. Removing the negative vibration is what spiritual cleansing is all about. You must learn to cleanse yourself spiritually and protect your home and work place from these unwanted visitors.

I have clients that come to me for cleansing including; psychologists, other psychics, and especially Reiki practitioners. It is sad that they forgot the basics of cleansing themselves after every healing session. They forget that they pick up their client's condition and sometimes the practitioner passes these on to others whom they come in contact with. That is why some patients come in for a healing and come out feeling worse.

When it comes to cleansing yourself spiritually, I recommend using white sage because it is great for purification cleansing. You always start from the top of your head and work your way on down after every healing or therapy session.

I also recommend using the smudge sticks to cleanse and purify the home and every room within the home from the basement to the top floors. In the workplace, the practitioner should cleanse and purify between every healing or therapy session.

There are other products that you can use for cleansing. In another booklet, I will go into detail about how to cleanse yourself, your home, and your office. We will be offering workshops on this subject in the near future.

The following items can be used in cleansing:

Smudge Stick: I use the smudge stick to cleanse negative energy and emotion that the client may bring with him. I purify my healing center between healing sessions, and I also use the smudge stick to purify my body, home, and even some gifts that I may receive from clients and friends. The *Smudge Stick is used for protection and purification.*

White Sage: The white sage has the same vibration as the Smudge Stick but the energies are lighter. I like using white sage to call in my personal protective spirit, who serves as guide as well as guard to help cleanse my aura and body from any negative vibrations that I may pickup spiritually. *White Sage is used for protection and purification.*

Frankincense: Frankincense is used for cleansing the home, body, aura, and environment of all negative influences. It is wonderful for attracting the higher beings of light, which can influence your surroundings. Frankincense also helps to improve communication with the spirit. *Frankincense is used for protection and purification.*

Myrrh: Myrrh helps to purify the area, raise the vibrations, and creates peace and harmony. However, myrrh is seldom burned alone. It should be mixed with frankincense to promote the manifestation of the forces attracted by the incense blends. These open the astral doorway to the spiritual world and attract the archangel's forces. *Myrrh increases spiritual awareness and uplifting.*

Incense cones, loose incense, and stick are common and can be purchased in almost every place in the world. Sandalwood, Jasmine, Dragon's Blood, Rose, Cinnamon, Sunflower, Joop, and High John can also be used. I have named just a few of the incenses that I enjoy burning from time-to-time.

PUTTING IT TOGETHER

Seichim Healing Session:

You have learned some of the basics of Seichim. Obviously you cannot learn everything from this compact booklet. But having the basic means you are off to a good start. Seichim is a journey of SELF-discovery and by following the guideline in this booklet and with regular use you cannot go wrong. TRUST your inner guidance, listen to the spirit within, your Higher Self.

Working with the patient:

- Start off with a short prayer and call Light to you.
- Next, open the four upper Chakras, the Crown, Third Eye, Throat, and Heart, for you to receive all of Seichim energies.
- Take a few deep breaths, and breathe Light into your heart, opening the heart and allowing the heart to expand throughout your being.
- This is a must: ask your patient's permission to perform the healing.
- The patient should be seated or lying down with his eyes closed and body relaxed enough to receive the Seichim's energies of the angels.
- After you call in your healing guides to channel the Seichim energy through you, you should be standing behind the patient with your arms and

hands extended, waiting to receive the energies of the healing guides and spirit doctors.

- Once an attunement is made both with spirit doctors and the patient, you will be able to receive intuitively the diagnosis of the cause and counsel how to assist in overcoming the symptoms of the problem.

- Follow your intuitive self; your Higher Self and a team of spirit doctors will guide you.

- At times you, the practitioner, will experience the patient's symptoms in your own body. This is common.

- Remember to cleanse the aura first, before you begin the healing.

- Start from the top of the head and move downward to the sides of the body, cleaning the aura. *(You should always sweep in a downward motion, NEVER UPWARD).*

- Raise your hands above the head, hold the hands apart, with fingers extended and separated. Start bringing your hands down slowly and gradually along both sides of the body, (feeling the aura) until you are able to feel something different, like a cold spot. Just follow your intuitive self.

- Intuitively you will be led to where your hands should be. At all times you must remember your Higher Self is guiding you.

- At times you will be guided to touch the ailing part of the body, whether that be the head, chest, arms, or any special parts of the body. You will feel enormous amount of heat coming from the palms, and you will feel tingling sensations coming from the fingertips as the spirit channels Seichim energies into the ailing part of the body.

This is a sure sign that the healing is taking effect.

- Keep your attunement on the spirit within, as your spirit doctor assist you in the healing. Do not worry about small details. "Am I healing the right way?" or "I hope the healing is taking." Such thoughts will break your concentration on the healing energies. *Always remember, God is working through you.*

- At times you will see white light flashing from your body into the patient which is the Seichim energies coming from the Source God All-That-Is that dwells within YOU.

- When you feel the Seichim energies starting to slow down, then you know the healing is coming to an end. Then you must stop when you no longer feel the energies enter into the patient's body and give thanks to the Source.

- Some patients may need some moments to re-adjust to the world after a Seichim healing session.

- Encourage the patient to give thanks to the Source for the healing.

- After the Seichim healing session you must close down your chakras and again give thanks to the Source for channeling the Seichim energy through you.

- Your energy will be high and you will feel like a glass of champagne, sparkling all over. This is a normal feeling after a Seichim healing session.

- ***Remember, always to clean your aura spiritually, after the Seichim Healing Session.***

After the Seichim session, the patient will feel inner peace and upliftment. At times the patient will feel lightness in the head, which causes the patient to sit motionless for a short period of time. This usually lasts from 30 seconds to two minutes. At other times the patient will display enormous amounts of happiness. This lightness and uplifted feeling should be anticipated, enjoyed, and encouraged.

Give thanks to God for the Seichim energy that flows through you. Then thank your Healing Guides for using you as a channel to re-establish life energy back into the body of your patient.

My Master Teacher

"Everybody should be a channel, we all have the capability of channeling our Higher Self and learning from our Higher Self. Man must wake up to the fact and start using his Divine Self."

My Master Teacher

THE AURA

What is an Aura?

*T*he aura is the visible part of the electromagnetic force field which surrounds the human body, and it reflects the subtle life energies from within the physical body, and much more. It is God, Universal Love, and Light that hold billions and billions of cells and molecules together in the physical body. The aura is a reflection of the spiritual self and the physical body. It is these energies that are affected by our thoughts and life style. If you are feeling ill, the aura will reflect ill health or any other condition that you may be having. The aura will display symptoms long before the physical body starts to signal that a problem is beginning. A Seichim master or a healer can observe this in the aura either as dull or gray in color. If a mental condition is present the aura will reflect the disharmony within the aura.

The Seichem master, with the guidance from their healing angels, can go in the aura field and remove those blocked areas that are causing the problem to the physical body. After the adjustments, the healing angels can bring harmony and balance to the aura and the physical body. You must remember this, "Whatever the spirit or the physical body is feeling, it will automatically reflect in the aura field."

Around the physical bodies are the etheric double, a narrow band of energy that outlines the body. The etheric body double is usually no more than a half an inch outside the skin of the physical body. The aura can expand, generally, from about one foot to three feet and beyond.

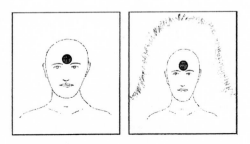

Focus your attention on the third eye.
Gently raise your eyes above the hairline to see the aura.

How You See The Aura?

- The person should be sitting or standing in front of you about 10 – 12 feet away.
- Close your eyes and call light in.
- Take a few deep breaths to relax the body.
- Look at the person right between the eyes in the middle of the forehead.
- Don't stir, but gently look in the middle of the forehead.
- Now, focus your attention on the person's third eye in the middle of the forehead for a few moments.
- Now, raise your eyes slowly above the person's head.
- Look at the outline above the head; you will see light extended from the head, and as you move your eyes downward toward the shoulders, you will also see the light extended from the body.
- Yes, that is the aura of the person.

You should be able to observe the aura; if you are not able to see the aura the first time, try again and again. A true Seichim Master Teacher can empower you to increase your vibration to help you to see the aura. Once the eye is activated it is up to you to practice and keep the energy flowing. At first you will feel a tingling sensation in the middle of your forehead, which will cause tears in the eyes of some students. This is normal.

BALANCE THE CHAKRAS

*I*t is my intention to save the student some time and labor by providing the lesson that I learned over the years from my *guides and master teachers*.

First you need to become completely relaxed. I want you to sit with the spine erect, feet flat on the floor, eyes closed. Relax your mind and body. Take a few deep breaths, and feel the vital force flowing in your body. Now, take a few more deep breaths and release all tensions and anxieties outward and upward to the light.

Balancing the chakras is easy; just relax and have fun. If possible, ask a friend to guide you through balancing the chakras. If that is not possible, record your own voice, reading the following instructions on a cassette tape before you begin these exercises.

As you become completely relaxed, I'm going to count from one to 10 and on each number that you hear, I want you to become more and more relaxed and more peaceful with your inner self.

Beginning to count:

1. You begin to feel so very relaxed.

2. All of your cares and concerns are behind you now.

3. You feel yourself becoming more and more completely relaxed.

4. Any noise you may hear is a signal for you to go deeper and deeper.

5. Totally relax and feel yourself going deeper and deeper.

6. I want you to visualize a white light surrounding your entire body from the top of your head and down to your feet.

7. Feel yourself going deeper and deeper into your relaxation.

8. Now feel yourself feeling totally relaxed.

9. Imagine or feel your *master teacher's* coming to assist you in balancing your chakras.

10. We are going to balance the seven major chakras: There are also over 300 minor chakras, but we are going to work with the seven major chakras centers.

The chakras are energy vortexes that appear as tiny spinning wheels or dish-like shapes that hold the etheric body in the physical body. The chakras extend about one quarter to an inch from the physical body. I want you to visualize each chakra one at a time.

The first chakra is called the **Base** chakra and it is located at the base of the spine. I want you to visualize a red color, a bright and beautiful red color. As you see the color red, I want you to take your hand and imagine that you are removing all the blockages from the Base chakra. As you are removing the blockages from your Base chakra, I want you to use your breath and breathe out and release all the debris from these areas and make room for new energy to flow in. Now, imagine as you inhale with each breath that you are sending Seichim energy to the Base of the spine and energizing all areas of the **Base** chakra. Now feel the Seichim energy flowing within the Base chakra, and flow with it. This energy comes from the Universal Consciousness.

The second chakra is called the **Solar Plexus chakra,** or sometime called the Naval chakra. It is located just above the Base chakra. I want you to visualize this round disk-like shape as a bright yellow color shining forth from this area of the Solar Plexus. As you see this yellow disk-like shape, I want you to take your hand and visualize that you are removing all the debris and blockages from this area of the chakra. As you are removing the blockages from your Solar Plexus charka, I want you to use your breath and breathe out and release all the debris from this area and make room for new energies to flow in. Now, imagine as you inhale with each breath that you are sending Seichim energy to the Solar Plexus chakra and energizing all areas of the Solar Plexus chakra. Feel the Seichim energy flowing within the Solar Plexus chakra and feel your Solar Plexus becoming more and more active, alive, and well-balanced.

The third chakra is called the **Spleen chakra** and it is located just above the Solar Plexus. I want you to visualize this round disk-like shape as a bright orange color shining forth from this area. As you see this orange disk-like shape, I want you to take your hand and visualize that you are removing all the debris and blockages from this area of the chakra. As you are removing the blockages from your Spleen chakra I want to use your breath and breathe out and release all the debris from this areas and make room for new energies to flow in. Now, imagine as you inhale with each breath that you are sending Seichim energy to the Spleen chakra and energizing all areas of the Spleen chakra. Feel the Seichim energy flowing within the Spleen chakra, spinning and expanding, becoming more and more active. This is the memory of the astral journey.

The fourth chakra is called the **Heart chakra** and it is located just above the Spleen. I want you to visualize this round disk-like shape as a bright green color shining forth from this area. As you see this green disk-like shape, I want you to take your hand and visualize that you are removing all the debris and blockages from this area of the chakra. As you are removing the blockages from your Heart chakra, I want you to breathe out and release all the debris from those areas and make room for new energies to flow in. Now imagine, as you inhale with each breath, sending Seichim energy to the Heart chakra and energizing all areas of the Heart chakra. Feel your heart becoming more alive, more abounding, and expressing a Universal Love and true compassion for all humanity. The heart is the chamber where you pursue the Master Presence within the center of your Being.

The fifth chakra is called the **Throat chakra** and it is located just above the Heart. I want you to visualize this round disk-like shape as a bright blue color shining forth from this area As you see this blue disk-like shape, I want you to take your hand and visualize that you are removing all the debris and blockages from this area of the chakra. As you are removing the blockages from your Throat chakra, I want you to breathe out and release all the debris from those areas and make room for new energies to flow in. Now imagine as you inhale with each breath, sending Seichim energy to the Throat chakra and energizing all areas of the throat chakra. Feel your Throat becoming more alive and balanced. Your Throat chakra is the communication center; it is the bridge between two worlds, man and spirit.

The next chakra is called the **Brow chakra or the Third Eye.** This chakra is located at the center of the forehead. I want you to visualize this round disk-like shape as a bright indigo blue color shining forth from this area. As you see this indigo blue disk-like shape, I want you to take your hand and visualize that you are removing all the debris and blockages from this area of the chakra. As you are removing the blockage from your

Third Eye chakra, I want you to out and release all the debris from those areas and make room for new energies to flow in. Now imagine, as you inhale with each breath, sending Seichim energy to the Third Eye chakra and energizing all areas of the Third Eye chakra. As you send Seichim energies to this area, you are awakening your third eye center. Flow with the feeling; it is the energy of GOD.

The seventh chakra is called the **Crown chakra,** and this chakra is located at the top of the head. The Crown chakra radiates a brilliant violet color. I want you to visualize this round disk-like shape as a bright violet color shining forth from this area of the Crown chakra. As you see this violet disk-like shape, I want you to take your hand and visualize that you are removing all the debris and blockages from this area of the chakra. As you are removing the blockages from the Crown chakra, I want you to breathe out and release all the debris from those areas and make room for new energies to flow in. Now imagine as you inhale with each breath, sending Seichim energy to the Crown chakra and energizing all areas of the Crown chakra. Now I want you to feel your Crown chakra becoming more and more open and more alive as you awaken this center as it is your direct link to the Universal Consciousness, wisdoms, and perfection of complete faculties.

As you come out of your altered state, remember to close down your chakras and give thanks to the Source.

THE SEVEN CHAKRAS DIAGRAM

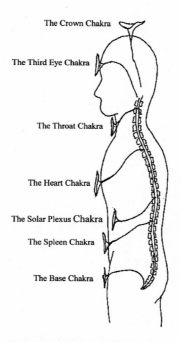

The Crown Chakra

The Third Eye Chakra

The Throat Chakra

The Heart Chakra

The Solar Plexus Chakra

The Spleen Chakra

The Base Chakra

BASIS ENERGY WORK

*T*here are seven major chakras, three masters and four major, which are attached to the spinal cord and the nervous system. There are also over 300 minor chakras that are located all on certain parts of the body.

It is my intent to show the student how he can open and stimulate his chakras and bring in more light and energies to his system. These exercises will help raise the Kundalini. The Base chakra is the ***master*** chakra and must be activated first. This chakra is the doorway for Kundalini energy to emerge.

The Kundalini has its own agenda; once the Kundalini is activated in the Base of the spine, it will flow naturally upward through the spinal cord to the top of the head, removing, healing, and cleansing any energy blocks in its way that may hinder its process. This brings on new awareness's, new abilities, clairvoyance, clairaudience, healing, channeling ...these are natural abilities that all of Gods children are born with. It is ***YOUR HERITAGE.***

Raising the Energy:

Before we get started on your exercise, you must enter in silence with intention to connect to your Higher Self and call light in, to help raise their vibrations and open the chakras.

Ask your Higher Self to help cleanse your aura. You should be standing for this exercise. Take a clear ***glass of water,*** three quarters full or stand in front of your sink, with the water running and imagine that you taking a shower. Cleanse yourself spiritually from the top of your head and sweep on a downward motion. Imagine all of the negatives that you may have picked up during the day are being washed way.

You should be sitting down for this exercise with your feet flat on the floor, as you bring your body to a relaxing state. Your mind should be clear of all worries and bring your awareness to Mother Earth. Feel the vibration of the earth and ask Mother Earth to energize you. Now, draw upon Her ***"love, power, strength and light,"*** and allow yourself to be grounded and planted with feet deep into the earth spiritually.

Mentally I want you to become aware of your breath and use it as tool to draw on Mother Earth energies to help open and stimulate the chakras.

With your eyes closed, become one with Mother Earth and feel her love and ask permission to use her energy. Wait until you begin to feel her vibration. Now, draw in the energies from Mother Earth into the Base chakra. On the inhaled breath, draw the energies up into the Base chakra in your spine and hold it for a few moments. Then, on the exhale breath, breathe light into the Base chakra. Do this a few times. The amount of energy you draw from Mother Earth will help open and stimulate the Base chakras and awaken the Kundalini energies. The energy that you will receive from Mother Earth will help stimulate your chakras and transform into a different level. This transformed energy will then flow into your subtle bodies, energizing your chakras. You will actually feel the Kundalini energies tingling and surging up the spine and removing blockage on the way up to the Crown chakra on top of your head.

Chakra Stimulation:

Opening the chakras: I want you to visualize your chakras as a beautiful sunflower that extend from your body. Take your right hand and imagine that you are opening these lovely flowers, gently. To achieve this you must focus your awareness in the area of a chakra, using the mind and hands to manipulate the chakra. If you cannot visualize the chakras just know that they are there. Put your right or left hand over the areas of the chakra, and just feel like you are doing it. It is that simple.

Now I want you to use your awareness of the breath and breathe light into the chakras. Use your hand in a circular motion over the chakra, as you send more light to stimulate the chakras. Pull the energies from Mother Earth up your spinal cord into the chakras. On the inhale breath, hold it for a few moments...then exhale, breathing light into the chakras.

1. **Base chakra:** is the *master chakra* and the *most important one to activate.* Pull the energy up from Mother Earth, into the Base of your spine. Mentally use your mind and hand to open the Base chakra. Use your breath and breathe light into the Base chakra, at the same time using your hand to send light in a circular motion to open and stimulate this chakra. Repeat this seven times. The more you practice this exercise you will start to feel heat and energies building up in the base of your spine. This will be the Kundalini energy. You must remember this. "It is important to use your mind and visualize or imagine the Kundalini energies rising up from the base of your spine and travel through your spinal cord, into the chakras centers. Remember, whatever you see in your mind eye or feel, it will happen."

2. **Spleen chakra:** Pull the energy from Mother Earth into the Base of the spine, up the spinal cord into the Spleen charka. Use your hand and mentally send light into the spleen chakra to open and stimulate it. You will feel the heat and energies starting to vibrate as the Kundalini rises up the spinal cord into the Spleen chakras centers. The Kundalini will cleanse and remove any blockage that it may encounter on its way up the spinal cord.

3. **Solar Plexus chakra:** Pull the energy up from Mother Earth into the Base of the spine. Now, feel the Kundalini moving up the spinal

cord into the Solar Plexus chakra. Use your hand and mentally send light into the Solar Plexus chakra and stimulate it. You will feel the heat and energy rising up your spine into the Solar Plexus chakra.

4. Heart chakra: This is one of the Main chakras. Pull the energy up from Mother Earth into the Base of the spine. Now, feel the Kundalini moving up the spinal cord into the Heart chakra. Use your hand and mentally send light into the Heart chakra and stimulate it. You will feel the heat and energy rising up your spine into the Heart chakra. Your Heart chakra will generate enormous amounts of energy and expand through out your being.

5. Throat chakra: Pull the energy from Mother Earth into the Base of the spine and up the spinal cord into the Throat chakra center. Use your hand and mentally send light into the Throat chakra to open and stimulate it. You will feel the heat of the Kundalini energies rising up your spine, cleansing and removing emotional problems as it travels up your spine into the Throat chakra.

6. Third Eye chakra: Pull the energy from Mother Earth into the Base of your spine. Now feel the Kundalini energies moving up through the spinal cord into the Third Eye in the center of the forehead, between brows. Use your hand and mentally send light into the Third Eye to open and stimulate it. You will feel the Kundalini energies rising up your spine, cleansing every cell in your body as it travels up into the Third Eye chakra.

7. Crown chakra: This is one of the Main chakras. Pull the energy from Mother Earth into the Base of your spine. Visualize or imagine the Kundalini energies moving up the spinal cord and exiting out of the top of your head. Breathe Seichim energy into the Crown chakra center and stimulate it. You will feel the Kundalini energies mixing with the Divine energy above your head and showering over the body. You will feel an awakening of your spiritual centers and your natural abilities will appear—healing, clairvoyance, clairaudience, channeling, and the gift of knowledge as the Kundalini release and cleanse your system.

Note: After the energy work you must remember that it is very important to close down your chakras. Take your hand and raise it above your head, and bring your hand down in front of you in one sweeping motion. Mentally say to yourself, "I am closing down all of my charkas." Just know that it is happening. Whatever you think, so be it. Remember, you are the *master* of your temple.

When I first started raising the Kundalini energy and developing my chakras, it took couple years on and off to develop any kind of sensation. Practice will develop the chakras, but the offshoot will find your psychic abilities developing naturally.

Warning:

If student wants to awaken the Kundalini, he needs to seek out a true Seichim or Reiki Master Teacher who has the understanding and knowledge of these matters. The knowledge had been guarded for years without clues as to the order in which the Kundalini should be passed   through the charkas. For this reason alone any student's trying to awakening the Kundalini without a qualified practitioner or Master teacher may pose serious dangers. Please exercise caution. You are dealing with extremely powerful energies.

RAISING THE KUNDALINI

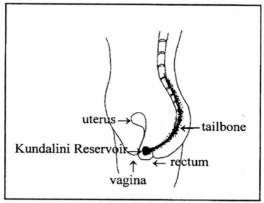

The diagram above is to help the student raise his Kundalini by looking at the illustration and observing how the Kundalini can be raised through the spinal column.

F irst bring your attention to the Kundalini reservoir and the tailbone. Now, become friends with this illustration and imagine this is a part of you. Close your eyes and feel the Kundalini reservoir, and then visualize the Kundalini starting to rise up your spine. Feel the warmth of the Kundalini as it starts to travel up the spinal column and into the Base chakra, the Spleen, Solar Plexus, Heart, Throat, Third Eye and the Crown chakra.

Note: When you use this technique, whatever you think is your reality, it will happen. Remember, you are the master of your Temple, your mind and body will follow your will. It is that simple.

CHAKRAS ENERGY CENTER

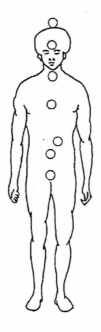

THE HUMAN BODY

*T*he chakras function like a computerized storage battery: These centers are points of Energy that extend from the body that take in, store, and release the life force that the body needs to function and is directly related to the way we live and what we are like a person.

WHITE - CROWN

Objectivity, Understanding, Connection with the Higher Self or the God-Self of the I AM Presence, Spirituality.

Blockage creates lack of judgment and understanding

VIOLET - THIRD EYE

Insight, Knowing, Intuition, etc. Connection with the Astral Plane. Psychic Precept.

Blockage creates lack of intuition, imagination.

BLUE - THROAT

Communication; manifesting our personality, Inner Self. Bridge between two worlds, man and spirit.

Blockage creates Introversion, lack of personality.

GREEN - HEART

Higher Emotions; Love, Unconditional love, Compassion, relations with others and the Universe.

Blockage creates lack of feelings, anxiety, and coldness.

ORANGE - SPLEEN

Memory of astral journeys. The painter, artist, poet etc… Creative force. Feelings.

Blockage to the nervous system cause disharmony.

YELLOW - SOLAR PLEXUS

Physical phenomena, Lower emotions, Telepathy, Astral Projection.

Blockage creates inability to deal with emotions.

RED - ROOT

Sexuality, creativity male & female aspects of Self. Seat of the Kundalini.

Blockage creates lack of confidence. Fear of others.

THE HOLY BREATH

*B*efore you begin any spiritual exercise, you need to established peace and calmness in your body. To do this, you need to practice spiritual breathing. My *master teachers* call it the "Holy Breath." What is the "Holy Breath?" Prana is the principle of life, which is found in the air, earth, water, food, etc. It is the universal energy that is in everything and is everywhere. It is Seichim, the Living Light and the vital force that flows through your body. It is the breath of life. So when you consciously take in these vital energies with your breathing, you are taking in an abundance of GOD energies.

Sit or lie down and clear your mind. Take a few deep breaths and feel yourself breathing. Breathing rhythmically, inhale and exhale slowly, filling the lungs up with God's vital energies. Now, breathe naturally and focus your whole attention on breathing. As you bring your awareness to your breathing, your mind is occupied, allowing it to think on a much deeper level. It is the breathing that will help bring you into an altered state. It is that simple.

Exercise for using the Breath and seeing the inner Light

The Holy Breath always helps you enter your altered state.

1. Close your eyes and relax your body.

2. Call light in and open your chakras up.
3. Take a few deep breaths and breathe slowly, filling the lungs.
4. Now breathe rhythmically and naturally, as you focus your attention on the Third Eye.
5. Feel the body becoming more and more relaxed and calm.
6. Continue to focus on the Third Eye.
7. As you focus on the Third Eye, breathe light into your Third Eye.
8. You will feel the energies starting to build up in your Third Eye.
9. As you inhale you will feel your body absorbing the vital energy, filling and energizing every cell in your body.
10. Feel the energies rising up from the charkas, directed to the Third Eye
11. You should start to feel some pressure in the middle of your forehead.
12. Keep your attention on the Third Eye, not stirring, just watching the activities as they start to take place in your Third Eye.

Regardless of what color light you see, always try to pierce it with your insight to see beyond, and you will see in many dimensions! With this knowledge, you can use this method of watching your breathing to bring the mental activities and the life force under control with practice.

Remember to breathe and practice the sacred breath, every day or every other day until it becomes natural to you.

Breathe rhythmically to bring in the energy of God. Seichim energy is the greatest gift you can give yourself. Seichim are vital energies and essential for you to exist and function in your physical body. That is why my *master teachers* named it the "Holy Breath," for it helps transmute and release the negative energies in the body. It will also help balance and enhance the chakras and cleanse and expand the aura. Practice your breathing exercises until they come natural to you.

PREPARATION OF AN ALTAR

*T*he first step you need is to locate a place in your home that has no or little traffic. You can place the altar in the bedroom, basement, or attic. This will be your special place where you will come and worship in peace. An altar is only a focal point. The true altar lies within the chamber of the heart where God is.

Preparing an altar

The second step is that you must begin to **cleanse the area** where the altar is to be placed, including, **the walls, floor, and the table.** You are creating a sacred space for yourself where you will enter in your meditation and seek your God.

Altar set-up

You can set your altar up on the floor, bench, desk, on top of your dresser—any flat surface or table will do. The size does not matter, as long as it is adequate enough to arrange the items on the altar and have easy access to them. My guardian angels revealed to me how I should set my altar up.

The table should be covered with white linen, with two vases of flowers, one on each side of the table. The flowers must be fresh; the color should be pastel, light in color (pink, white, yellow, orange etc.) You will need three white candles, arrange in a triangle, with a glass of water in the middle of the triangle. The spacing of the triangle should be about 18" apart. You also need an incense holder with incense and a matchbox.

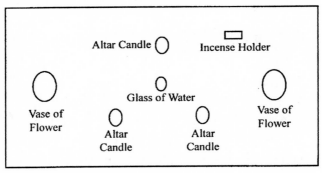

Tools:

- Two vases for fresh flowers.
- Three white altar candles.
- Three candleholders.
- A goblet half full with water.
- An incense holder for sticks, cones, or powder incense.

The meanings of the altar set-up:

- The pastel colors are persisting colors, which indicate movement for life, which is always moving and growing, never being held back.
- The fresh flowers indicate growth and life.
- The three candles represent the Trinity, *(The Father, Son & the Spirit)* which makes the triangle.
- The candle flames represent, God, All-That-Is and GOD said, "Let there be Light." "So it is."
- The water means purity, a vital life force.
- The burning of the incense indicates communication.
- The white linen also represents purity.

DECLARING AFFIRMATIONS

*T*his affirmation is a very powerful affirmation; it helps to activate the Soul's remembrance of who you really are. *"God Is I AM and WE are One."* When the mind cannot calm down and the chatter persists. Then you begin affirming over and over again: *"God Is I AM and WE are One, God Is I AM and WE are One, God Is I AM and WE are One."* Your affirmation will lead you into a deep meditation; take note of the inner wisdom of the Source of All Wisdom when you connect to your God-Self.

A PRAYER OF GUIDANCE

*G*od is the source of all my supplies,
He answers my every need.
I am a divine child of God and I should be fulfilled
As I become an instrument of his Divine Light.
I will be guided daily
For that which is right and perfect to me
That I may have happiness and support
from this time forth.
Thank you Father. So be it!

The Power of You
Affirmation, repeat three times:
I AM *your name,* and I will.
Meaning:
I AM that I Am God of *your name* and I will do the will of God. This affirmation is a very powerful one, because it is using the power of GOD, also the power of YOU. Remember, "God Is, I AM and WE are ONE".

Prayer:
Thank you Father for this day that you have given to me to use in your service.
Meaning:
It speaks about the power of God, that power have given you life and for that life, you owe service. And if you are to serve God you can only serve God by serving man.

WORKSHOP AND EVENTS

BEGINNERS AND ADVANCED STUDENTS
SEICHIM Healing Workshop
Saturday, 1:00 - 3:00 P.M. (Workshops $20.00)

This is an on-going educational Seichim development workshop. Come and immerse yourself in the Seichim Living Light Energy and deepen your unique connection to the Light as it flows through you. It can manifest itself many ways in your life, such as increased healing abilities, clairvoyance, and artistic talents. We will discuss and educate participants, through demonstrations and exercises in the following areas: Seichim/Reiki techniques, meditation, balancing the chakras, aura, working with your guardian angel, master teacher and more...

Workshops are intense

Maurice has a unique gift of opening his students' Third Eye, to enhance meditations and recall dream states. It is not uncommon to actually experience a spontaneous healing during this workshop.

SEICHIM/Reiki Certification

You will be taught this ancient healing technique in a single weekend, from beginning to Master level. 11 A.M – 4 P.M.. Includes Master Level Certificate upon completion. $400.

If you are interested in making an appointment for a **Seichim Healing session** e-mail or call for an appointment.

For Seichim/Reiki Certification schedule and registration, write, call or e-mail for information.

House of Miracles Healing Center
12235 Marcel Lake Estates
Dingmans Ferry, PA 18328
Tel. 570-828-1996
houseofmiracles@pikeonline.net
www.houseofmiracles.net

Please call to reserve a seat, as space is limited. Sessions begin promptly. Plan to arrive five to ten minutes in advance of the starting time.

SEICHIM/REIKI CERTIFICATION

Learn about the ancient art of Laying on Hands. Help others to heal themselves and experience your own self-healing. (Group or private instructions.)

Maurice Ramsey will teach you the traditional and the non-traditional Seichim system, a form of natural healing that has been around since the beginning of time.

Seichim I Practitioner $125.00

- What is Seichim and how does it work?
- Introduction to your Guardian Angels
- Empowering and attunement
- Opening the Third Eye and the Heart Chakra
- Energy fields, auras, and Chakras
- Pendulum
- Meditation

Seichim II Practitioner $125.00

- Introduction to your Healing Guides
- Attunement
- Calling Living Light Energy
- Connecting with your Higher Self
- Meditation
- Empowering and working with water
- Scanning the Aura
- Healing

Seichim III Master Teacher Practitioner $350.00

- Attunement
- Meditation
- Practice
- Distance healing
- Spiritual cleansing
- Raising the Kundalini (For those that are ready.)

CERTIFICATION GIVEN AT COMPLETION

Bargain package: Pay $400 at the time of level I, and Level II and full Mastership are included in this one price. Represents a $200 savings.

ABOUT THE AUTHOR

M aurice Ramsey is a well-known Spiritual Healer and a certified Seichim/Reiki Master Teacher in the Seichim Method who incorporates traditional and non-traditional classes in Seichim. He is the founder and director of the "House of Miracles Healing Center." Maurice is in every sense of the word, a "True Healer." When Maurice prays and connects to the spirit within for God's Divine healing energy to flow through him, you can see a beautiful white light that radiates around his head and hands as he goes about his healing work.

Maurice has been a gifted healer since childhood. At age ten he realized that he had been blessed with an unusual gift and has dedicated much of his life to developing his healing skills. Maurice knows there is an intelligent force behind the healing process, and through the teachings of his *guardian angels, master teachers* and *healing guides,* Maurice was able to strengthen his healing skills.

As he has grown spiritually, he realizes and states, "Whether it is Spiritual Healing, Reiki, Therapeutic Touch, Crystal Healing or any other kinds of healing, all healing comes from God and God is Spirit, and all healings are spiritual in nature. **NO MAN HEALS. GOD HEALS THROUGH MAN.** The healing angels are always ready to assist the healer in his work. It is they, (Spirits), who in God's name, use their wisdom and the forces at their command to work through the healer to take away pain, to loosen locked joints, to rebuild tissues, and to bring peace and harmony back to the body."

BIOGRAPHY: Maurice Ramsey is an ordained minister and has been active in Spiritual Healing for over thirty-five years. He is also a certified Seichim/Reiki Master Teacher. Maurice holds a Doctorate of Metaphysical (MsD) and a Doctorate of Theology (TD). Maurice's story made the national news, in the *Times Herald Record's* "Hands that Heal" (August 6 1997). He has been quoted in the local newspaper on several occasions for his Intuitive Readings.

BENEFIT FROM SEICHIM

- Enhances effectiveness of traditional medical treatments.
- Seichim/Reiki healings compliment and work with the medical profession, especially before surgery.
- Helps speed up the recovery time, even after surgery.
- Is known to increase the healing process.
- Help to loosen locked joints and rebuild tissues.
- Reduces stress and relieves chronic illnesses
- Helps to balance the body.
- The healer provides specific information to facilitate the healing process.
- Intuitive guidance.
- Helps eliminate chronic pain.

How do I contact Maurice?

You may write to:
Attn: Maurice Ramsey
House of Miracles Healing Center
12235 Marcel Lake Estates
Dingmans Ferry, PA 18328
Call (570) 828 1996.
Or email: houseofmiracles@pikeonline.net
www.houseofmiracles.net

HEALING TEMPLE OF LIGHT MEDITATION

*M*editation can help improve your energy level, health, and general happiness while reducing stress and anxiety. Also, the more you get into the habit of meditating daily, you will feel your body being energize and looking youthful. There are many healing meditation techniques. One of the techniques that I have developed over the years for my students is called the Healing Temple of Light.

Before you begin to meditate you need to relax your mind and body, bring it to a peaceful, relaxing state within yourself. Then you invite God to come into your heart and mind. As you do this, you will feel warm vibrations; this is the presence of God within the center of your being. Fix your attention at the point between your eyebrows and feel a warm feeling within your heart center. As you begin to feel His Presence as a beautiful white light within, become one with the light. Contemplate God's attributes; God is all- loving, all-powerful, marvelous, and all forgiving. Rest in the silence of joy of just being in His Presence. After you become attuned to Seichim, the light of God, he will send forth his angelic healers to assist you in healing your self. Ask God to touch your spirit and help heal your body or whatever problems that you may have. The healing angels will hear your prayers, come to your aid, and diagnose your problem and begin to use Seichim the

Living Light to heal every cell and molecule of your body

As you go deeper into the stillness of your meditation, you can see the Seichim energies as a bright, beautiful white light that radiates all around you. Out of the Light emerge the angelic healers as they go about their healing work, unblocking those areas that are causing discomfort, taking away pain, loosening locked joints, rebuilding tissues, bringing peace and harmony to the body.

It's plain and simple, *you must always ask God to enter into your heart and mind* to touch your spirit and helps heal your body. You will feel God's divine healing powers flowing within and through your body touching and healing every cell in your body.

EXAMPLE

Sit with your eyes closed. Adjust your posture so you feel comfortable, putting your hands in your lap, facing up. Then take a few deep breaths.

Now I want you to imagine your entire body feeling relaxed, starting with your feet, calves, thighs, then up into your abdomen, lower back, chest, and shoulders. Next, relax your arms, hands, neck, and face. Do this until you feel peaceful and physically comfortable.

Adjust your posture so that your energy can flow more easily up and down your spine. Take few deep breaths and breath slowly.

Fix your attention at the point between the eyebrows and asked God to come into your heart and into your mind.

Ask GOD: "Please help me make a stronger connection to my Higher Self." Imagine that you are being joined by many Higher Beings of Light who are sitting in a circle around you. Feel the peace, joy, and love all around you. These Beings are here to assist you in meeting your Higher Self.

Imagine your Higher Self in the distance, beginning to come toward you. You might picture your Higher Self as a beautiful, shimmering, radiant light, greeting and welcoming you. Ask your guardian angel also, to assist you in making a stronger connection with your Higher Self. Feel the radiance of your Higher Self's love surrounding you and embracing you.

Now imagine your Higher Self taking you by your hands and transporting you to the Healing Temple of Light, to help heal and balance your body.

Feel yourself in the Temple of Light, as your Higher Self direct you into the room of liquar of Light. Bathe within the Light and feel all your troubles and pains washing away.

You are in your true "spirit" form and you feel the Seichim energy being sent to your body and you see your body is being healed on all levels.

You realize that you are an extension of GOD and that you are ONE

You may stay as long as you like in the Healing Temple of Light. When you come out of your meditation you will feel fully awake and healed. Thank God and your Higher Self for your healing.

As you come out of your meditation feeling healed, open your eyes say this affirmation: "God is Divine Love and Divine Love is now flowing through and around me, God's Divine Love is healing me right now, So be it."

Remember, that you are an extension of GOD. Keep that realization in your mind, feel it, and Know that you are an extension of the Living God that dwell within you. Whatever you want, just sit down and meditate on it, make your dreams into reality. I am not talking faith,

I'm talking about knowing that you have the power within you. So make it happen!!!

A SECOND CHANCE

As a Seichim Master Teacher, many people come seeking my help for what aliments they may be suffering, especially when the medical profession has said, "We're sorry, there is nothing else we can do for you." God always provides alternative approaches to healing when everything else has failed. There's always a second chance with the Source (God). No doors remain closed. You have the key to faith, and faith comes by knowing that God is the Source. As a rule, the Healer has to deal with those who have suffered for many years and who have received every conceivable kind of treatment, injections, radiation treatment, operations, and so on. They have come to the end of their rope. In these extreme cases, a Seichim session is able to help.

I am not a medical doctor or a specialist in the medical field; I do not prescribe remedies, vitamins, and the like. I am a Seichim Master, a vehicle for God's healing energy to flow through me, to help the poor in spirit who are suffering from some sort of pain, stress, fatigue, chronic illness, etc. The Seichim Master, through the aid of God's healing angels, or your Higher Self, is able to touch the soul of the patients and bring peace and harmony to the mind and body of the patient. You must also realize not all that are sick can be healed by a healer, there are spiritual laws at work, and there are some patients the Seichim Master can't help even though there's healing on some levels that they are not aware of.

God always hears prayers and sends forth His healing angels to assist the Seichim Master, diagnose the problems of the patient and transmit the Seichim energies through the healer to the problem areas of the patient's body. The angels are always ready to help to assist the healer in his healing work. The whole reason for healing is to touch the soul of the patient who is ready to awaken the physical body to be healed. Then the healing will help ignite the divine spark that can grow and illuminate and strengthen the body. This is always the purpose behind the working of the Seichim healing energies.

The sick man, who is healed when all other avenues were closed is the best living testimony to the spirit of God's power. He recognizes that he has been brought face to face with a power greater than anything he has encountered on earth.

Seichim the Living Light and prayers compliment and work with the medical profession especially before surgery. Seichim helps speed up the recovery time even after surgery Seichim is known to increase the healing process. One day the medical profession and the Seichim Master will work hand and hand helping the sick recovers much faster than conventional ways.

There is no magic or quick solutions when it comes to healing. Just know that the Father that dwells within you does the healing. Remember, not all healing takes place immediately. There should be follow-up Seichim sessions, until all conditions are cleared up.

A MESSAGE FROM SPIRIT

I received this message from Aventgento; his earthly name at that time was Joseph, some 2000 years ago. He is the father of Jesus the Christ. This message was channel through the medium Cerver. I had the greatest honor of knowing them both. I received wisdom and counsel from Aventgento, for the over 16 years that I knew Cerver.

"I shall do the work in the face of God in front and I shall use my hand with Jesus behind. I shall walk straight ahead to the sun ahead and with the moon behind and all the stars behind me are dreams, little gifts, and I shall believe in my heart what is within, as I am here with my God and shall serve you and man."

9/17/83
Aventgento

NEWSPAPERS ARTICLES

SUNDAY RECORD
April 6, 1997
HANDS that HEAL

By LEIGH HURSEY
Staff Writer / Times Herald Record

At 6-years-old, Maurice Ezira Ramsey wasn't sure what he was doing when he put his hands on people. But his mother's friends and neighbors who complained of headaches or stomach pains continued to stream into the Ramsey's St. Nicholas Avenue apartment in Manhattan.

The little boy would simply touch people where it hurt and they reported feeling better. At first, Ramsey's "power" seemed questionable to his mother, Ernestine. She was glad her friends felt better, but maybe a cure existed only in their minds.

But one day as Mrs. Ramsey dressed one of her younger children for a doctor's appointment, Maurice, then 7, kept begging her to stay home. She planned to leave in the late morning on a bus bound for the Bronx. Maurice had never been clingy, so she began to pay attention to his pleas. "He held onto me," she said.

Mrs. Ramsey stayed home with Maurice. And that afternoon, about the time she would have been heading home to Manhattan, an elevated train was in a fiery accident. Her bus would have passed under the same tracks. "I said 'Oh my God, this (gift) is really true,'" she said. "It really shook me up." But she didn't encourage it. "At first I tried to hide it," Mrs. Ramsey said. "Back in those days people were skeptical of those things."

But today more and more people are seeking alternatives or supplements to traditional medicine. And more doctors are recognizing the importance of the spirit in healing. Maurice is a 52-year-old minister ordained by the Virginia-based United Spiritual Scientist Fellowship. And in a two-car garage attached to his Cuddebackville home, he runs the House of Miracles. (The town's codes prohibit construction of a church on the property.)

A quiet, unassuming man with a slight stutter, Ramsey doesn't offer flamboyant healing demonstrations like some televangelists, although some of his sessions may be mentally intense. His Sunday services and workshops focus on meditation, self-discovery, and prayer. Ramsey divides his time between healing, and reading. At the direction of the Holy Spirit, he devised a set of 58 cards with Native American images and themes. He's a self-described clairvoyant and a medium through which God heals physically, emotionally and spiritually.

He cannot, and will not, take credit for strange or miraculous phenomenon resulting from a visit to his House of Miracles. "I don't have any control," he says. "I'm only a channel for the Holy Spirit to flow through me."

Although Ramsey's healing ritual remains virtually the same, the sensations felt by others vary. Ramsey starts with a prayer asking the Holy Spirit to enter his mind and body. Once he feels the energy coming into his head and heart and radiate from his hands, he brings himself into a light trance. His hands follow the outline of the body, hovering about an inch above.

"At times a person will tell me what's wrong. Others, I just know where to go." Ramsey said. As the person sits upright with closed eyes, Ramsey looks for cold places on the body that indicate blockages. When he finds a blockage, he places his hand on the spot and sends energy to that place. Some say they feel a sense of calm or see a light. Others compare the experience to feeling static electricity.

ALTERNATIVE SOURCEBOOK
November 2000
"Healing comes from within"

By: ROBERT CRAUSE
The Crause Column

The Reverend Maurice Ramsey Seichim Healer did not learn healing from books or earthly teachers. Through spirit Rev. Ramsey learned a variety of healing methods. At 2:30 am in the morning when the energy and atmosphere are still and calm Rev. Ramsey is taken to other planes of consciousness and taught healing arts. Ramsey stated "The spirit of God uses man as a vehicle for healing." When the attention is focused entirely on God the reverend can mentally invoke healing energies. This is being one with God. At this time healing takes place.

The Times Herald Record, The Poughkeepsie Journal and Sullivan County Democrat have done numerous features and articles focused on Reverend Ramsey his healing and predictions. When Ramsey was busy with the healing of the sick he was approached by a Journalist from the New York Times. Ramsey refused to be disturbed.

When Ramsey is involved with healings some people see a light surrounding Ramsey's head and hands. He is in a spiritual state and the healing work is of great importance. Ramsey was not irritated that the Journalist did not wait to get the interview. He has been approached by radio stations and various people of the media. His predictions for celebrities, sports stars and prominent people have been documented in articles and interviews.

Reverend Ramsey concerns himself predominantly and primarily with the art of healing the sick, terminally ill and serious medical patients.

He enjoys teaching others to meditate and help heal themselves. There are many people of the area who can benefit spiritually, emotionally, mentally and physically from Rev. Ramsey. The House of Miracles Healing

Center holds healing services and classes in Meditation, Healing, Yoga, Tai Chi Chuan, Reiki and much more. The House of Miracles exists to help people in need who want to learn and want healing and spiritual enlightenment.

I have read many of the feature articles in various newspapers praising Ramsey for his gifts and altruism also many personal letters and testimonials documenting the miraculous results of Ramsey's healings. I have also brought people to Ramsey who were amazed by his healings he would perform informally and spontaneous reading as the information came to him. A deeply religious associate of mine immediately referred to Ramsey from the time he met him as the Holy Man.

A couple drove 3 hours from Philadelphia, PA to receive healing. Jerry was concerned for his wife Sue who was terminally ill. Rev. Ramsey explained the Seichim session and performed the healing. Sue stated that she felt the vibrations and felt more peaceful then she had ever felt before. Tears of joy rolled down face. She looked around and told her husband "Everything would be all right." She thanked Rev. Ramsey and hugged her husband. Ramsey was then led to heal Jerry who suffered from severe arthritis. Five hours later Ramsey received a call from Philadelphia. Jerry stated that the first time in 5 years He was free from the pain in his knees and back.

I have met with healers and teachers in my travels and must say the Rev. Maurice Ramsey radiates peace, love and healing. To see the joyous results and the expression of relief and well-being on the face of those he has helped is a beautiful experience.

SUNDAY RECORD
November 1, 1992
Positive thoughts open doors

By JULIA CAMPBELL
Staff Writer / Times Herald Record

Middletown - The Rev. Maurice Ramsey splashed Rendon's Tabaco incense on his hands before he used them to clear the "negativity" from Joanne Smith's aura.

Taking deep breaths, Ramsey placed his hands above her head. Then moved them, trembling down the length of her body.

"You've got some blockage down here," Ramsey said as he passed his hands over her stomach and used his fingers to pull out the negative energy. "Ok, that's being released now. That's better."

Ramsey, a certified minister of the Light in the United Spiritual Scientist Fellowship and director of the House of Miracles in Cuddebackville, called on the spirit to help him heal Smith and five others at a holistic healing demonstration yesterday at Howard Johnson's in Middletown.

While the annual Psychic Fair went on next door, Ramsey showed participants how he heals. Holistic healing helps people harmonize their physical, emotional and spiritual bodies through stress reduction.

"There is no magic to this," Ramsey told them. "The power comes from within. I'm only a channel for the spirits." Ramsey said the healing only works for those who are ready to be healed, for those who are ready to be healed, for those who believe the Holy Spirit can heal.

Smith, herself a spiritual healer and minister of the Sanctuary of Light Church in Newburgh, volunteered to be   first.

"I just want you to know, I don't let many people work on my energies," Smith told Ramsey

But when he finished, Smith said she had felt the "tingling, I felt the light going through me."

Julie Trainor, 35, of Thompson Ridge told Ramsey she had problems with her stomach and head. It was her first holistic healing.

"Focus on the beautiful white light, pull it into your body, coming from the crown of the head through the body," Ramsey told her.

Within minutes, Trainor said she felt relaxed.

"I hesitated before coming here, but I'm glad that I did," Trainor said. She said she would do it again.

Ramsey said he has had the gift to heal since childhood, when he would heal relatives and family friends at his boyhood home in the Bronx.

While he dabbled in crystals at first, Ramsey turned to holistic healing after he injured his back from a fall at a construction site several years ago.

"The more I do it the stronger I get," Ramsey said after the demonstration. Ramsey said self-healing technique can be used at home, too—stand in front of the bathroom sink and imagine taking a shower, running your hands down the length of your limbs, brushing the negativity away.

"Think positive and flow within the white light," Ramsey said. "We all have the power within us. The key is L-O-V-E. With that you can open any doors."

THE TIMES HERALD RECORD
Ramsey sees into the future

Staff writer of the Times Herald Record
Date unknown

Most people already believe in the Holy Spirit, but there are exceptions like Hector Rodriguez of Manhattan. Although Rodriguez wasn't much of a believer in God, he went to Ramsey nearly seven years ago for a reading at his pregnant wife's urging. He met Ramsey a couple of years earlier through friends and was aware of his reputation.

Ramsey told Rodriguez his wife was pregnant and warned him to expect serious health problems with his newborn. But Ramsey assured him that she—he predicted the gender too—would recover.

Rodriguez's daughter Catega was born more than two months premature. Among other problems, she developed hydrocephalus, an accumulation of fluid in the brain. Doctors told the Rodriguez' Catega could end up with cerebral palsy or mental retardation.

With the exception of a delay in walking, some trouble counting numbers in sequence, and a slightly drifting attention span, Catega is a normal 6-year-old girl. Rodriguez attributes her recovery to Ramsey's predictions and prayers.

"I'm a strong believer in God, stronger than ever before," Rodriguez said. Ramsey only started exploring healing seriously about 20 years ago. Once he became a teen-ager, Ramsey started to suppress his healing ability and the brief flashes he had occasionally foreshadowing events in even a stranger's life. The visions were frightening sometimes. He would involuntarily see dark images of, say, a car wreck.

He grew up to be a carpenter by trade and in 1977 he moved to Cuddebackville. A couple of years later his life was changed by an encounter he had with a voice and image he believed to be Jesus. He described Jesus' face as "white as a sheet." The voice encouraged him to open his eyes - not his physical eyes, but his spiritual eye.

The voice said, "You're a healer." Ramsey said "I want you to bring healing to my generation."

Seven other voices, he believed to be angels, reassured him they would be with him.

In this vision, he was shown a church too. He found the church—the United Spiritual Scientist Fellowship—accidentally as he was walking down Middletown's North Street days later. He started attending and eventually conducted healing services each Wednesday.

People flocked to the church and even his home. In 1990, he started the House of Miracles out of his home. Four years later, he added the garage for the House of Miracles. Inside the garage, a table with two vases of silk flowers, a round glass container of water and three candles sits at the end opposite the door. A stool sits in front of the table and a few stackable chairs are situated in a semi-circle.

Ramsey doesn't charge for healing, but he accepts donations. Gifts are determined by the visitor, whatever they can afford. The donation could be $1 or $100. The workshops on self-healing, spiritual development, and guardian angels that Ramsey holds mainly in the spring and summer range in cost from $10 to $65, depending on the length and intensity.

A few times the healing is instantaneous. Ramsey claimed that a young boy who walked with an obvious limp ran—free of limp—from the alter of the North Street Church. Some are not healed at all.

And he never advises that people abandon conventional medicine. Because he doesn't keep track of successes, he depends on feedback that may come in a phone call or letter from the people who believe he helped heal them. He doesn't keep track of the numbers of people he's seen or healed, but Ramsey estimates he has seen more than 3,000 people, excluding hundreds more in churches.

"It takes a certainly quality to be a healer. And that's love," Ramsey says. "This a true love I have for my fellow man and I can't explain it."

Ramsey can be reached at The House of Miracles, 570-828-1996

TESTIMONY LETTERS

Dear Maurice,

This is to thank you for your insight and extraordinary ability to see into the future on behalf of my daughter Catega.

There have been numerous occasions when you have used your gift for me, but in particular your predictions in the past five years have been appreciated. My daughter Catega (your goddaughter) has been a prime example. Before she was born, I asked you for a reading and you explained to me that she would be born with medical difficulties but not to worry. She would overcome these problems and pass through this life as well as any other or better.

Of course I remained the skeptic. How could you possibly know ahead of time of what was to be?

On March 11 1991 Catega was born. Three months premature 2 pounds 3 ounces. She was in the Neonatal Intensive Care Unit at New York hospital for more than 2 months. The problems were massive and at times (for myself) overwhelming. She was born with brain bleed, developed hydrocephalus, meningitis, and a heart murmur among other problems.

She had a VP shunt installed into her head (plastic tube inserted through her brain into her abdomen); this was done at least 9 times (in one year) due to clogged tubes. She was on constant medication for various diseases, since she was newborn and had not developed her immune system.

To see my daughter in such a state, seeing these machines registering her conditions, left me in tears. To see her heart rate go to astronomical levels, and seconds later down to zero, was despairing, I was almost at the point of giving up hope.

My wife Pat and myself did the best we knew how. We slept at the hospital, sang songs, and read stories each day to her and drilled the doctors and nurse for information and updates. This was a trying time for us both, a time in which I grew as a Human Being.

Catega is now 5 years old, she is a charming young girl that overcame enormous problems (physical and learning) and is on track.

So I ask again, How is that you knew ahead of time of what was to be?

Maurice you have a gift. I am no longer the skeptic I use to be. Again I thank you for your prayers and the healing that you gave to my daughter.

Yours truly,
Hector Rodriguez
New York, NY

Dear Maurice,

In January of 1985, I was diagnosed with a disease called Sarcoidosis. There's not much known about this disease. What I can tell you is that can be treated, but not cured. It is also known to attack the organs of the body. In my case, the disease attacked my lungs, building scar tissue, leaving me very short of breath and exhausted all of the time.

At the time I was diagnosed, we were a military family with all of the best doctors and hospitals at our disposal. I was constantly back and forth to the Naval Hospital in Bethesda, Maryland, for tests and consultations, with hordes of doctors at my bedside. I had it all – removal of lung tissues, poking, squeezing, different treatments, and medications. After all of that, I was depressed. Then one day someone very close to me suggested I go to Rev. Ramsey's House of Miracles…it couldn't hurt, I said to myself the doctors had tried everything else, I thought, if I went with an open mind, it might help. Actually, my experience that evening was uplifting. It was wonderful. I'd never felt such a sensation before. During meditation my entire body was tingling and I felt as light as air. I cannot describe the sense of peace that come over me.

I went back to House of Miracles Healing Center three times after that incredible session and every time I left there, I'd feel more energized as my disease was slowly dying away. Today I am very thankful to Rev. Ramsey for my healing and above all I thank God, because my disease is now in remission.

Sincerely,

S. Gray

Cuddebackville, NY

Dear Rev. Ramsey,

When my friend first told me about the "House of Miracles," my thoughts were very skeptical and I figured that it was just another one of those advertisements where the guy is claming to make your life better by paying $200 to tell you stuff you already knew.

When I finally decided to take my chances, I realized that I was all wrong about him. Before I had gone, I was stressed out and just always in a bad mood. When I had a Seichim session, I felt so much better, as if he took all my pain and bad thoughts from me. The healing showed me that I don't have to worry about everything, and just to be happy and let things happen. I've been following his advice and everything has been great.

K.S.
Port Jervis, NY

Printed in the United States
23145LVS00001B/184

9 781932 047967